Grizzly Riddles

by Katy Hall and Lisa Eisenberg

pictures by Nicole Rubel

PUFFIN BOOKS

PUFFIN BOOKS
Published by the Penguin Group
Penguin Books USA Inc., 375 Hudson Street, New York, New York 10014, U.S.A.
Penguin Books Ltd, 27 Wrights Lane, London W8 5TZ, England
Penguin Books Australia Ltd, Ringwood, Victoria, Australia
Penguin Books Canada Ltd, 10 Alcorn Avenue, Toronto, Ontario, Canada M4V 3B2
Penguin Books (N.Z.) Ltd, 182–190 Wairau Road, Auckland 10, New Zealand

Penguin Books Ltd, Registered Offices: Harmondsworth, Middlesex, England

First published in the United States of America by Dial Books for Young Readers,
a division of Penguin Books USA Inc., 1989
Published in a Puffin Easy-to-Read edition, 1996

1 3 5 7 9 10 8 6 4 2

Text copyright © Katy Hall and Lisa Eisenberg, 1989
Illustrations © copyright Nicole Rubel, 1989
All rights reserved

The Library of Congress has cataloged the Dial edition as follows:

Hall, Katy. Grizzly riddles.
Summary: An illustrated collection of riddles and puns about
grizzly bears, such as "Why can't grizzlies sing the high notes?
They're all bear-a-tones!"
1. Riddles, Juvenile. 2. Grizzly bear—Juvenile humor. 3. Puns and punning.
[1. Riddles. 2. Puns and punning. 3. Grizzly bear—Wit and humor. 4. Bears—Wit and humor.]
I. Eisenberg, Lisa. II. Rubel, Nicole, ill. III. Title.
PN6371.5.M396   1989   818'.5402   86-29275

Puffin Easy-to-Read ISBN 0-14-03.8028-0

Printed in the United States of America

Except in the United States of America, this book is sold subject to the condition that
it shall not, by way of trade or otherwise, be lent, re-sold, hired out, or otherwise
circulated without the publisher's prior consent in any form of binding or cover
other than that in which it is published and without a similar condition
including this condition being imposed on the subsequent purchaser.

Reading Level 2.3

What do little girl grizzlies wear in their hair?

Bear-ettes.

What would you get
if you crossed
a grizzly and a kangaroo?

A fur coat with pockets!

What baseball team do grizzlies root for?

The Cubs!

What kind of fish
do grizzlies like to catch?

Bear-acudas!

What do you call a nice, cheerful, friendly, helpful grizzly?

A failure.

Why can't grizzlies
sing the high notes?

They're all bear-a-tones!

What happened to
the grizzly skater
who fell through the ice?

She became a blue-bearie!

Who is a grizzly's favorite funnyman?

Grrrrrrrowl-cho Marx!

Where do grizzlies
sit on airplanes?

Anywhere they want to!

Why didn't the grizzly walk on the gravel road?

She had bear feet!

What time is it
when a grizzly wakes up
from his nap?

Time to run!

What is bigger than a grizzly but lighter than a feather?

A grizzly's shadow.

Why did the grizzly cross the road?

It was the chicken's day off.

Why can't a grizzly keep a secret at the North Pole?

His teeth always chatter.

What happens when a banana sees a grizzly?

The banana splits.

What grizzly stands in the middle of New York Harbor?

The Statue of Lib-bear-ty!

What time do grouchy grizzlies get up in the morning?

At the crank of dawn!

What weather is even worse than raining cats and dogs?

Drizzly grizzlies!

Who won the
grizzly beauty contest?

No one.

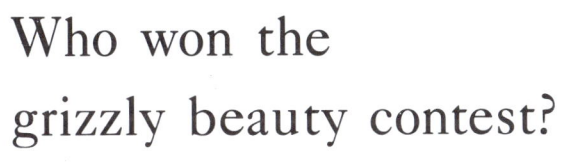

Where do grizzlies come from?

Bear-izona!

What sport
do grizzlies love?

Picnic basket-ball!

When grizzlies make a pie, what do they like to put in it?

Their teeth!

Why was the grizzly so smart?

She just ate a whole school of fish!

What do you call
a bear with a new perm?

A frizzly grizzly!

What Broadway musical do grizzlies like best?

My Bear Lady

Why do *you* look like
a grizzly cub
when you take a bath?

Because you're a little bare!

Why did the grizzly tip-toe through the campsite?

He didn't want to wake up the sleeping bags!

Why do grizzlies have such sticky hair?

They use honeycombs!

What would you do
if a grizzly sat in front
of you at the movies?

Miss most of the movie!

Which grizzly
is the ringleader?

The first one in the bathtub.

What would you get
if you crossed a grizzly
with a dog?

    A neighborhood without any cats!

What sound do grizzlies make when they kiss?

Ouch!

What do you get when a grizzly walks through your vegetable garden?

Squash!

Is it true that a grizzly won't attack you at night if you carry a flashlight?

It all depends on how *fast* you carry it!

Why don't grizzlies spend much time in front of a mirror?

They can't bear it!

What should you do if you see a great big, hungry grizzly?

Hope he doesn't see you!

What country
do grizzlies like
to visit in the winter?

Den-mark!
It's known as the Hi-Bear Nation!

What muscleman do grizzlies most admire?

Conan the Bar-bear-ian!

How many campers
can a grizzly eat
on an empty stomach?

Just one—
after that his stomach isn't empty!

What grizzly has bad breath, long, yellow teeth, mean little eyes, and needs a bath?

A perfectly normal grizzly!

Who is the only one
that remembers grizzlies
at Christmas?

Santa Claws!

What do bears think of these jokes?

They think they're just grisly!